# The Gift That Keeps Giving!

Plant a Seed and Watch it Grow

Makiya Turman

Plant a seed & Watch it Grow
Walk with me
Water me
Watch me Flow
Nourish my soil
Feed my Soul
As I burst open, Let me Bee
Surprise, I am transformed & free
From Life to Life, I'm living like new
My experience changes & I've grown to feed you

Planting a seed and watching it grow is a beautiful experience. It is amazing to observe the process of life.

Your gardening experience will become a personal journey. Keep your eyes open to fully experience the natural process of life and see how we are one. Let nature direct you as you prepare the environment to plant your seed in.

To first prepare is to care. However, just making the decision to start this journey exhibits care. From my experience the gardening journey prepares and cares for you along the way. It made me wonder who is nurturing who? I have my answer to that question.

Start your journey to find out.

TAKE NOTE OF HOW YOU FEEL RIGHT NOW BEFORE YOU START YOUR
JOURNEY. YOU MAY WRITE DOWN YOUR THOUGHTS TO REFLECT ON LATER.

_____

_____

_____

_____

_____

_____

_____

_____

When you seek to bring life into the world you intend to create a better future. As you plant your seed you accept the responsibility to provide for and nurture it. Nature plays a big part along the way.

Take the time to watch your seed transform. Pay attention as the seed opens, comes out of its shell and springs forth out of the darkness into the light. In life our environments change and just like a seed we adapt beautifully.

Quench my thirst
Warm me up
Let the wind blow
And I'll erupt
You see my root
Now I must grow up

Through me nutrients
travel
Up my Stem
I am strong
I am grounded
Absorbing food from below
So my leaves up top can
grow

Photosynthesis begins
I'm taking the sunlight in
Let's transform
Watch me produce
Take care of me & I'll do
wonders for you

Some tips from my personal gardening journey:

1. The seed knows what to do.
2. You are not in control just a participant.
3. Less is more.
4. If you start you will succeed.
5. It's all part of the process.
6. Enjoy the ride.
7. It's Already Done!

## Phase 1: GET READY!

??? Think about what type of seeds you want to use.

Heirloom, Hybrid, Organic, GMO, Open-Pollinated
I recommend Heirloom seeds. It's the gift that keeps on giving abundantly.

??? Think about what you want to grow.
Tomato, Potato, Greens, Beans, Lettuce, Cucumbers, Cilantro, Parsley, Flowers, Herbs, Fruit

You can also think about what you like in your salad and create a Garden Salad.

Write down what foods you enjoy to eat regularly. If you have limited space this will help you determine what you should grow.

_____

_____

_____

_____

_____

_____

_____

_____

_____

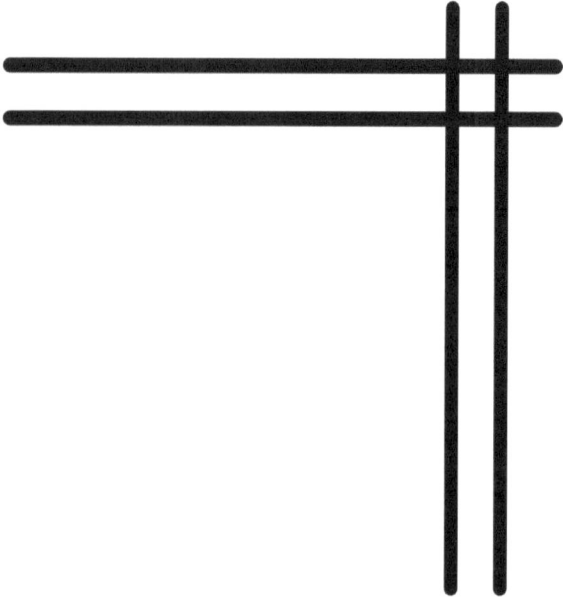

I love to plant something new just for the experience to see if it will grow. You will never know unless you try!

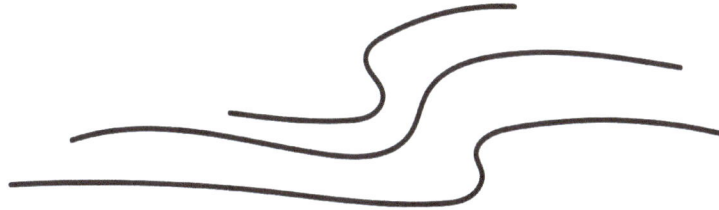

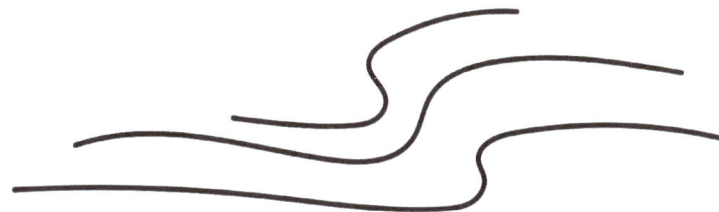

Once I tasted a homegrown tomato I had to start a garden. I have been hooked ever since. Gardening is a journey that you will enjoy experiencing more & more as you grow.

Make sure to plant some! From my experience they practically grow themself. Just water regularly & let the sun shine.

If you have not experienced a homegrown tomato get one and try it today. Find a local gardener or farmers market and enjoy. Now of course you do not have to try a tomato but if you have never had homegrown produce try something. It will change your life.

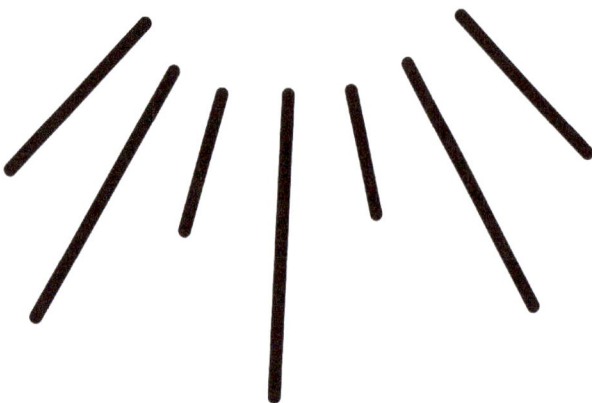

# Write down the thoughts that come to mind after eating homegrown produce.

What did you try?

_____

_____

What was your first thought?

_____

_____

What was your first question?

_____

_____

Did you enjoy it?

_____

_____

_____

# For everyone that has been enjoying homegrown food. Think back to your first experience. What sparked your gardening journey?

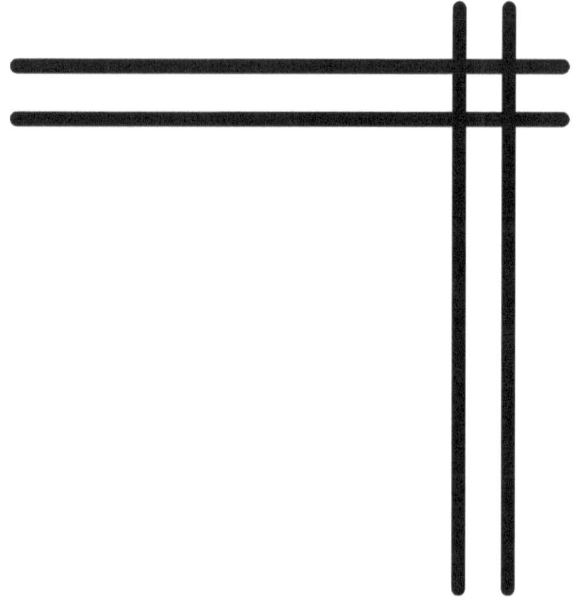

**Let your journey begin.**

Think about where you want to grow. Do not complicate this step. You can grow in just about anything and you do not need a lot of space to do it.

My garden has changed so many times since I first started many years ago. I first started in ground and over time I incorporated many techniques including raised beds, standing raised beds, fabric pots, old car tires, recycled containers & more.

The beautiful thing about gardening is you are the creator. You can do whatever you desire.

My first garden was in-ground. I grew a variety
of plants all from heirloom seeds. I must say
everything grew very well.

Make sure to add natural repellant
plants like Marigolds and  Petunias.

Take some time & visualize your garden. Write down or draw your ideas here.

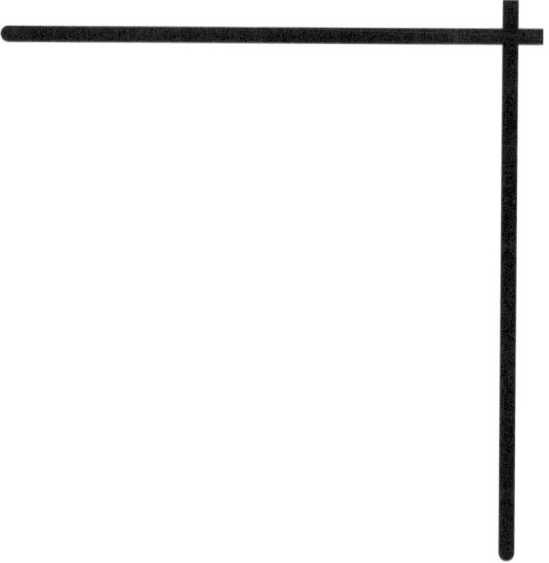

# Open your mind and be creative. There are many different ways to grow food.

**Raised Bed**

**Grow Bags**

**Cinder Blocks**

**Tire**

**No Dig Paper Barrier**

**Containers**

??? Think about when is the best time for you to get started.

Check for your last frost date according to your zone to make sure you start your seeds or transplants at the right time. The weather can have set backs so make sure the overnight temperature is predicted to be consistently above freezing.

A quick internet search will help you find this information for your zone.

**Note**: There are some cool season crops that can tolerate frost.

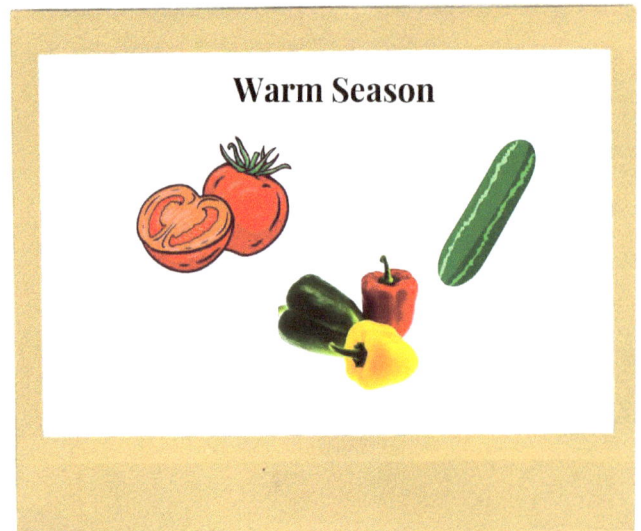

**Cool Season**

**Warm Season**

# Feeling hesitant? Just buy a pack of seeds.

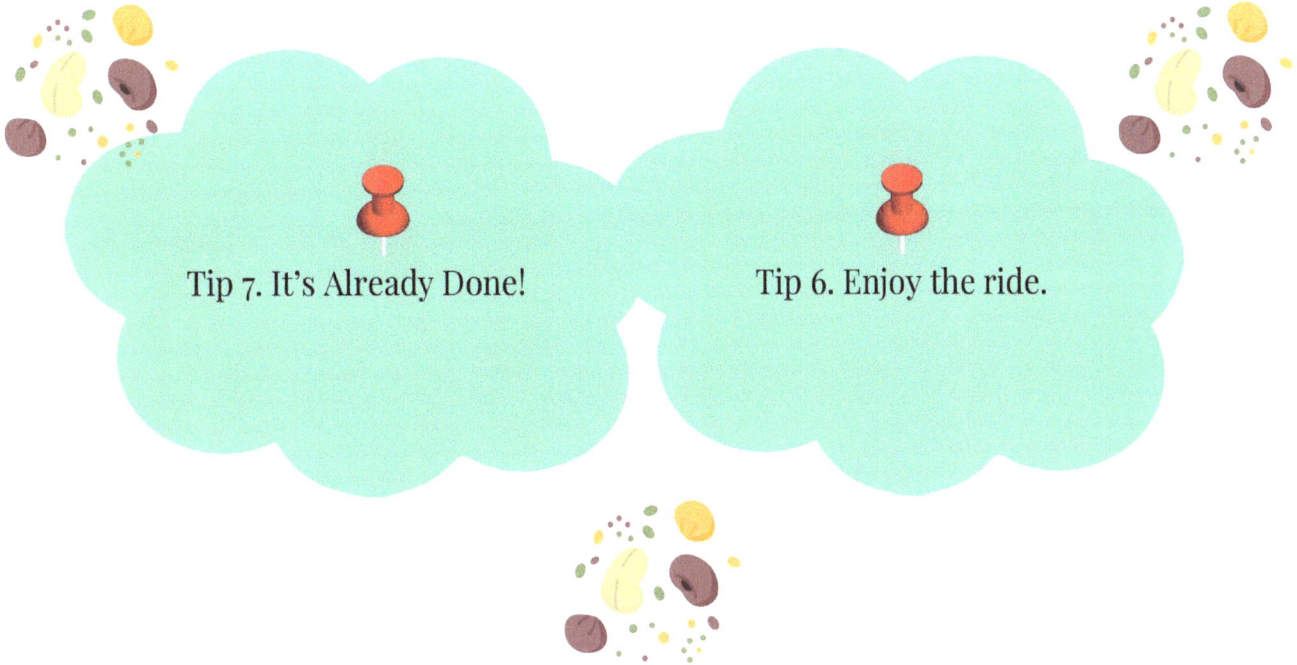

Tip 7. It's Already Done!

Tip 6. Enjoy the ride.

Now that you have completed the Get Ready Phase. Let's get **SET**. Well, this part is simple. Place your seeds in the environment you have chosen.

Plant

Nurture

Grow

Tip 5. It's all part of the process.

Tip 4. If you start you will succeed.

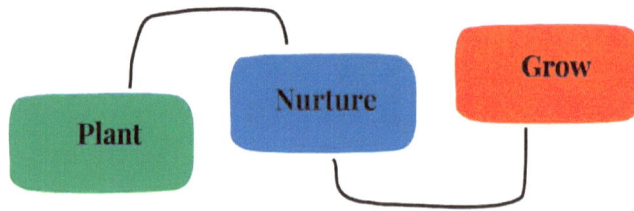

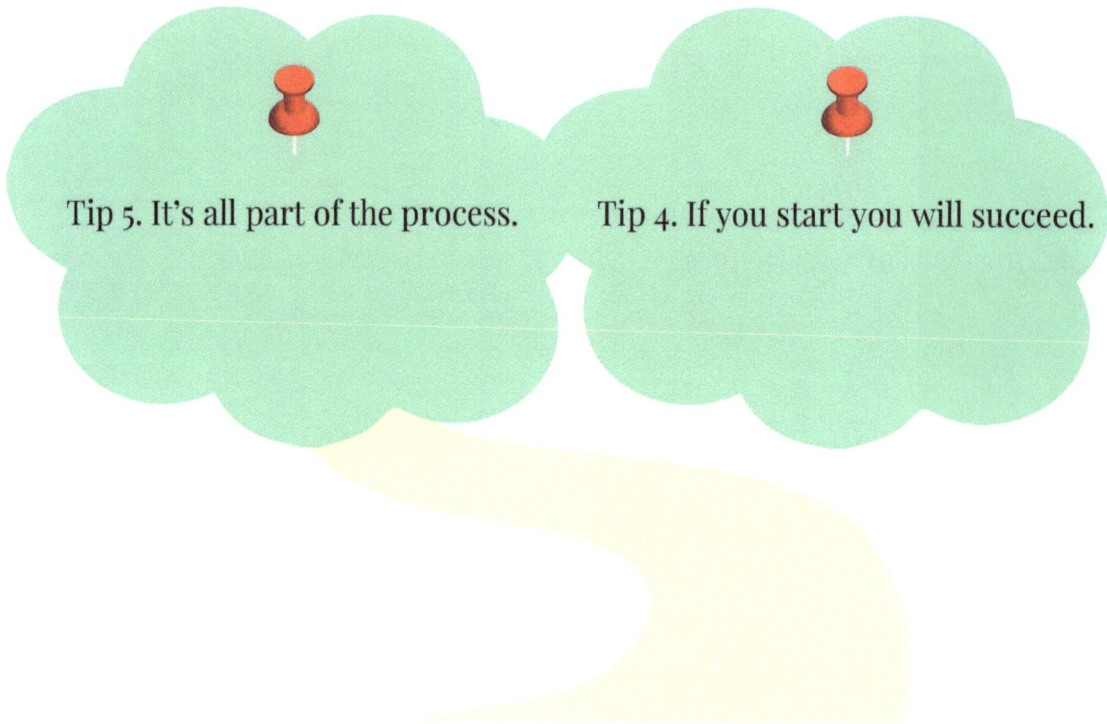

Use the chart on the next page to help you keep track of what you planted. Check the seed packet for spacing & depth instructions.

# Input the date & the name of the seed you planted in the chart.

| | | | | | | |
|---|---|---|---|---|---|---|
| | | | | | | |
| | | | | | | |
| | | | | | | |
| | | | | | | |
| | | | | | | |

# Watch it GROW!

Follow the directions on the seed packet for plant care.

**LEARN AS YOU GROW**

Use the chart to keep track of your plant growth and make note of your observations.

## WHAT DO YOU SEE?

| | | | | | | |
|---|---|---|---|---|---|---|
| | | | | | | |
| | | | | | | |
| | | | | | | |
| | | | | | | |
| | | | | | | |

Joining in on creation is a personal journey. Allow yourself to fully observe nature & the cycle of life.

Tip 3. Less is more.

Tip 2. You are not in control just a participant.

KEEP GOING, KEEP GROWING

Inside the seed is a map complete with directions to fulfill its purpose. Be fruitful and multiply.

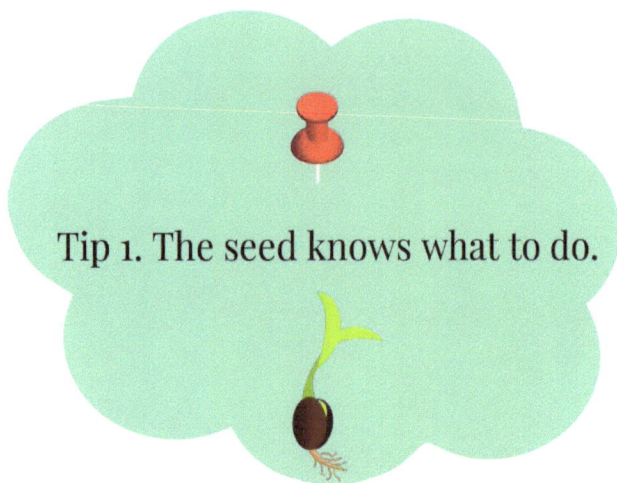

Tip 1. The seed knows what to do.

You will experience the collaboration & oneness of creation. Learn to release and be free in the moment to receive a message, guidance, and healing therapy specifically for you on this journey.

Nature is the gift that keeps giving abundantly from the seed within. You too shall be fruitful and multiply.

Best wishes on your journey!

Release and be free
Joy comes naturally
From nature you will see
What you perceive
If you observe
Natures course
All its curves
Structure, Sound, Safety
Healing & Growth
Discovery & Insight
Everything I carry in me

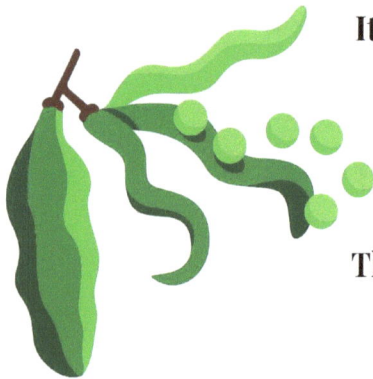

Peace
Be quiet
Be still in the dark
Its will is to develop & transform
Cozy, My home is warm
Wait, what's happening?
A disturbance I feel
Uncertainty, I'm ok!
Though something feels different
Curiosity
I'm breaking apart
It's so dark

My life is over
I am unable to see
Something is moving & guiding
me
Maybe I will survive
I will survive
I am getting stronger
Its like a tunnel
A path just for me
I see the light
I know what I am going to do
I am going to grow!

www.ingramcontent.com/pod-product-compliance
Lightning Source LLC
Chambersburg PA
CBHW060828270326
41931CB00002B/96